# THE SIERRA CLUB BOOK OF
# GREAT
# MAMMALS

Jonathon Scott/Planet Earth Pictures

## Sierra Club Books for Children
San Francisco

# THE SIERRA CLUB BOOK OF
# GREAT
# MAMMALS

Leonard Lee Rue III/Bruce Coleman Ltd

Mike Osmond/Auscape International

Written by Linsay Knight

Consultant Editor: Dr. George McKay,
          Macquarie University,
          Australia

Adapted from material supplied by:
Professor M. M. Bryden, University of Sydney, Australia
Professor M. J. Delany, University of Bradford, England
Dr. Valerius Geist, University of Calgary, Canada
Dr. Tom Grant, University of NSW, Australia
Dr. Colin Groves, Australian National University
J. E. Hill
Dr. Tom Kemp, University Museum, Oxford, England
Judith E. King
Dr. Gordon L. Kirkland, Jr, Shippensburg University, USA
Dr. Anne Labastille
Dr. Helene Marsh, James Cook University, Australia
Dr. Norman Owen-Smith, University of Witwatersrand, South Africa
Dr. Jeheskel Shoshani, Cranbrook Institute of Science, USA
Dr. D. Michael Stoddart, University of Tasmania, Australia
Dr. David Stone, Conservation Advisory Services, Switzerland
Ronald Strahan, Australian Museum
Dr. W. Chris Wozencraft, Smithsonian Institution, USA

The Sierra Club, founded in 1892 by John Muir, has devoted itself to the study and protection of the earth's scenic and ecological resources — mountains, wetlands, woodlands, wild shores and rivers, deserts and plains. The publishing program of the Sierra Club offers books to the public as a nonprofit educational service in the hope that they may enlarge the public's understanding of the Club's basic concerns. The Sierra Club has some sixty chapters in the United States and in Canada. For information about how you may participate in its programs to preserve wilderness and the quality of life, please address inquiries to Sierra Club, 730 Polk Street, San Francisco, CA 94109.

First Edition

Produced by Weldon Owen Pty Limited
43 Victoria Street, McMahons Point, Sydney, NSW 2060, Australia

Library of Congress Cataloging in Publication data is available from Sierra Club Books for Children, 100 Bush Street, 13th floor, San Francisco, CA 94104

Printed in Singapore

10 9 8 7 6 5 4 3 2 1

Page 1: A puma makes its way across the shimmering snow. It is an endangered species.
Page 3: Impala find safety in numbers.
Opposite page: It's hard to believe these huge humpback whales feed on tiny shrimp-like krill.
Page 6-7: African elephants on the move. In times of drought, it is the oldest female that leads the herd to food and water.

# Contents

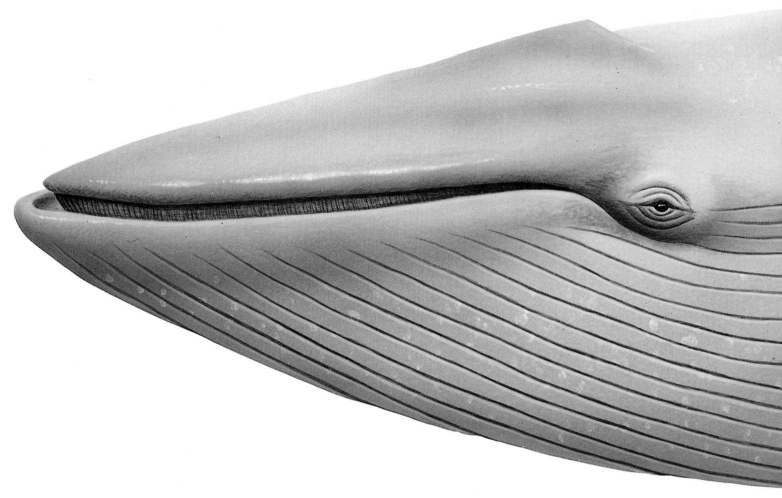

# What Is a Mammal?

Mammals are members of the animal kingdom. The word "mammal" comes from Latin and means "of the breast." The mammary gland is another name for the breast. Mammals are animals that feed their young with breast milk.

Mammals aren't the largest group of animals. The largest group by far is the invertebrates (animals without a backbone) — 95 percent of all the animals we know are invertebrates. Mammals belong to the much smaller group called vertebrates (animals with a backbone). Other vertebrates are fishes, amphibians, reptiles, and birds.

All mammals are warm-blooded, which means that their body temperature stays more or less the same no matter how hot or cold the surrounding temperature is. Animals such as snakes (reptiles) and frogs (amphibians) are called cold-blooded. Their body is cold if their surroundings

are cold, but in fact they get quite hot after they have been sunbathing.

Mammals come in all shapes and sizes. There are about 4,300 different kinds of mammals. The differences between them are astonishing. They range in size from the tiny field mouse to the huge, sea-dwelling blue whale; from a mud-wallowing hippopotamus to a flying bat. Humans are mammals too. So are gorillas and other apes.

Mammals live in all sorts of places — some in burrows under the earth and some in the sea; some in trees and others in caves. They have different diets as well — some eat insects, some flesh, others graze on grass, and some,

David Kirshner

like the whale, feed on plankton. And look at the many different ways they have of moving around — swimming, flying, walking, stalking, hopping, running, and many more.

## Three ways to identify mammals

Firstly, mammals have bodies that are covered with hair or fur. Some have two types of hair: long hairs protecting the outside, and shorter hairs, or underfur, closer to the body. The hair or fur helps provide heat control by trapping a layer of air close to the skin. Since heat finds it hard to pass through the air and escape, the hair or fur helps the animal to stay warm.

Some mammals, such as whales, have very sparse hair. These animals rely more on their layers of skin to keep themselves warm.

Secondly, mammal mothers feed, or suckle, their babies with milk. The young attach themselves to their mother's teats, or nipples, which are on her front, sometimes in a pouch. The milk is all the baby mammals need until they are old enough to find food for themselves.

Thirdly, the lower jaw of mammals, which holds the bottom row of teeth, consists of a single bone. It forms a mobile joint directly with the skull and can move without the rest of the skull moving. The upper jaw is firmly attached to the rest of the skull and cannot move by itself.

Because mammals can breathe while their mouths are full of food, they can chew for as long as they like before they have to swallow. Other vertebrates that can't do this are forced to swallow their food whole.

# Three Groups of Mammals

Mammals reproduce in different ways — some lay eggs, some carry their young in a pouch, and some have a womb. Scientists divide mammals into three groups, depending on how they reproduce. The three groups are monotremes, marsupials, and placental mammals.

David Macdonald/Oxford Scientific Films

▲ *This female meerkat is standing up to suckle her young. The milk is on tap whenever the babies feel like having a suck. It is so rich in vitamins, minerals, and other important nutrients that the babies need no other food until they are big enough to find food for themselves. A meerkat is an example of a placental mammal.*

## Monotremes

Monotremes are mammals that lay eggs. The eggs have leathery shells a bit like a crocodile's eggs. The young hatch out and cling to the fur on their mother's belly. Milk oozes out of the skin where the milk glands are (monotremes do not have nipples). The babies are only about ½ inch (1 cm) long when they first hatch.

There are only three monotremes in the world — the duck-billed platypus and two kinds of echidna, also known as

## Did you know?

The African elephant is the largest mammal that lives on the land. The smallest is the little-known bumblebee bat. In the sea, the blue whale is the mightiest creature. In fact, it is one of the largest living things on Earth; only a few kinds of tree are bigger!

Of all the mammals, human beings probably live the longest, a few of us reaching 110 years. Elephants come next, sometimes living 70 to 80 years. Not so lucky is the male antechinus, a rat-like marsupial, which mates at 11 months, then dies.

The most numerous mammal is probably the brown rat. Countless millions live on the Earth, in nearly every habitat. On the other hand, there are only about 60 Javan rhinoceroses left in the wild today.

The Virginia opossum often gives birth to 20, sometimes 40, young ones at a time! The Indian rhinoceros averages only one baby every 4 to 5 years.

The African elephant has the longest pregnancy among mammals — about 22 months, or nearly 2 years. Some shrews are pregnant for only 12 days.

One kind of armadillo gives birth to sets of 8 or 12 babies — all identical!

One species of bat has a tongue longer than its head and body combined.

The human heart rate is about 70 beats per minute. The elephant's is much slower at 35, but the tiny shrew's heart pumps away at 800 beats per minute! A mouse's heart rate is in between, at 600 beats per minute.

The biggest noisemakers among mammals are the large whales, some of which make the loudest noises of any living thing. Their calls travel through the water for hundreds — some scientists suspect thousands — of miles.

the spiny anteater. These unusual animals are found only in Australia and New Guinea.

## Marsupials

Young marsupials grow inside their mother's womb, but they are born before they are fully developed. They climb up their mother's fur into her pouch, where there are nipples that supply the babies with milk. Some marsupials you might know are kangaroos, koalas, and opossums.

Marsupials live in Australia, New Guinea, and in North, Central, and South America.

## Placental mammals

Placental mammals have this name because the young grow inside their mother's womb, attached to a placenta by the umbilical cord.

The placenta is the organ that gives food and oxygen to a baby in the womb. It carries away any waste matter as well. This constant supply of food helps the baby to grow to an advanced stage before it is born. The placental mammal mothers have nipples that produce milk to feed their babies after they are born. This group of mammals is the largest and the best developed.

▲ This female western gray kangaroo is carrying its baby, called a joey, in its pouch. Even when it can move about by itself, the joey will return to this safe pouch to sleep and to travel, or when danger is near. A kangaroo is an example of a marsupial.

◀ The long-beaked echidna digs for earthworms with its finger-like snout. Echidnas are monotremes, an unusual kind of mammal that lays eggs.

▼ *Dimetrodon is one of the earliest and least developed of the synapsids, mammal-like reptiles that lived 300 million years ago. It had a large fin on its back and grew to about 10 feet (about 3 m) long. It lived in parts of what is now North America. As you can see, it is not much like the mammals we know today.*

# Mammal Beginnings

The story of mammals began about 195 million years ago. How do we know what the creatures who lived then looked like? As there were no humans living on the Earth in those days, we have to base our knowledge on the remains of animals and plants that were alive then and have been preserved as rock.

These rock remains are called fossils. The first mammal fossils dating from these early days are tiny, insect-eating animals that shared their world with the dinosaurs. In fact, before the dinosaurs died out, most mammals remained small, timid creatures that probably only emerged at night to hunt for food. Even the largest of them were no larger than a pet cat. Most of them ate insects, although one group that looked a bit like the rodents of today ate plants. It is only in the past 65 million years, since dinosaurs became extinct, that mammals of many different shapes and sizes began to appear.

The best known of the first true mammals are the morganucodontids. Fossils of these creatures have been found all over the world and show that they were very small. Their skulls were about an inch (2 to 3 cm) long and the total length of their bodies was about 5 inches (12 cm). You can tell from looking at their teeth that they chewed insects and from evidence of their good hearing and sense of smell that they probably hunted at night.

Alistair Barnard

▲ Cynognathus *was more advanced than* Dimetrodon. *By looking at fossils, scientists know that* Cynognathus *had mammal-like teeth and powerful jaws. What they can't tell from fossils is whether or not this creature had fur.*

◀ *Morganucodontids like this one lived about 195 million years ago. They were very small — about the size of a shrew — and are interesting because they are among the earliest of the true mammals.*

## Windows in the back of the head

Some of the largest reptile fossils that have been found, dating from 300 million years ago, had a pair of "windows" called temporal fenestrae in the back part of their bony skulls. We know that these reptiles (correctly called synapsids) were the first creatures that were like mammals because present-day mammals have a form of these windows in their skulls too.

Synapsids, or mammal-like reptiles, were the animals from which mammals gradually developed over the next 100 million years.

## The unusual mammals of South America

South America was an island continent until it eventually drifted north to join up with North America, so its mammals developed differently from those of the rest of the world. An important group that developed there is called the edentates. Strange members of this group were the huge, armored *Glyptodon* and a giant ground sloth. Present-day armadillos, sloths, and South American anteaters survive from this group of mammals.

# A Brave New World: After the Dinosaurs

Millions of years ago, the continents of the world were joined together as one mass of land. After the dinosaurs became extinct, about 65 million years ago, the huge land mass began to separate into pieces. These pieces drifted slowly apart and eventually formed the continents we know today. For a short time Australia and South America were joined to one another by Antarctica. Then they drifted apart to form separate island continents on which very different groups of mammals lived. During this time North America, Europe, and Asia were still joined to one another. This movement of the continents affected the development of mammals on Earth.

▼ Uintatherium *was one of the first large, plant-eating mammals. It was about the size of the present-day African rhinoceros. It looks unusual to us because of the three pairs of bony knobs on its head.*

Within 5 million years of the extinction of the dinosaurs, some important new kinds of mammals had developed. Some were like the modern meat-eating mammals (carnivores), with sharp teeth and powerful limbs with sharp claws. Others were large plant-eaters (herbivores) with large, flattened molars for grinding grasses and little hooves on the end of their toes to help them run faster.

Alistair Barnard

Alistair Barnard

## The spread of the grassy plains

About 40 million years ago, the climate of the world became colder and about a third of all the more primitive mammal families were wiped out. After this came a long period when the climate was very mild. This period, called the Miocene epoch, marked the high point in the development of mammals — more groups lived then than at any time before or since.

During the Miocene, the grasses that grew on the Earth spread to form great plains, which were perfect for herds of grazing animals to thrive on. Horses, deer, and antelopes lived there, as well as some strange animals with front legs longer than their back legs, and *Indricotherium*, the largest land mammal that ever lived.

The apes also appeared during this period, and a little later, about 4 million years ago, the first members of a group that were the direct ancestors of humans.

▲ *You can see by looking at* Glyptodon *that it is a relative of the armadillo. It was about the size of a small car.*

▼ Indricotherium *was like a huge rhinoceros. Its height was 18 feet (5.5 m) and it weighed more than 40,000 pounds (about 20 tonnes). This makes it the largest land mammal that ever lived.*

Alistair Barnard

Leonard Lee Rue III/Bruce Coleman Ltd

▲ The thick, shaggy coats of these musk oxen protect them from the Arctic cold.

▼ This two-toed sloth is doing what sloths do best — hanging from the trees of the rain forest.

Gary Milburn/Tom Stack & Associates

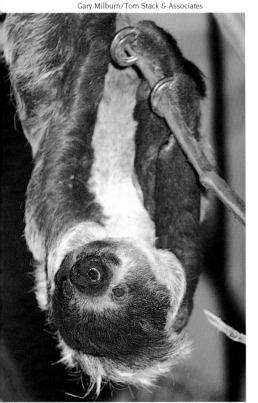

# Where Mammals Live

Mammals live in all parts of the world except for the central part of the continent of Antarctica. They have had to change in certain ways to enable them to live in many different places, such as tropical rain forests, grasslands, tundra, and deserts.

## Mammals of the forest

Trees are very important to mammals living in a forest. They provide food, shelter, places to hide, and means of escape. These forest creatures need to be able to move easily through the trees. In order to do this, some have developed a long tail that is like a fifth hand; some have big toes or thumbs that can move in a different direction from the others to help with climbing; and some move from tree to tree by gliding.

## Mammals of the grasslands

Speed is vital to mammals living in the grasslands. Long legs with hooves mean the animals can travel fast over long distances in search of food and water.

They are also good for running away from enemies. The maned wolf of South America doesn't have hooves, but it does have very long legs so that it can see over and move easily through the tall grasses of the pampas.

It is safer to live in a herd for a mammal of the grasslands. Animals such as lions and cheetahs tend to prey on a member of a herd that has fallen behind the rest. So by sticking with a herd, an animal is much safer.

## Mammals of the tundra

The Arctic tundra is a harsh place for mammals to live. It is a plain with no trees, where mosses, lichens, and dwarf plants grow. Caribou and musk oxen are two mammals that have adapted to the extreme cold of the Arctic. Smaller mammals, such as Arctic hares and foxes, turn white in the winter; this allows them to blend into the snow and escape their enemies.

## Mammals of the desert

Desert mammals have to put up with very little water and with temperatures that are very hot during the day and very cold at night. Most desert mammals sleep during the day in their burrows, where it is cooler and moister than on the surface, and come out at night. Animals that are active at night are called nocturnal.

Desert creatures eat seeds and insects, which nourish them as well as provide them with moisture.

Some large desert mammals, such as camels, cannot escape to burrows during the day, so they have developed other ways to cope with heat. One way is that their body temperature changes throughout the day to cool them.

# The bigger the feet, the easier it is to get around on the snow!

Skiers need their long skis to glide over the snow. Eskimos need large snow-shoes to move over the frozen wastes. Moving about can be just as difficult for the mammals of the tundra. Arctic hares grow fur on the pads of their feet to make them bigger. Caribou have very wide hooves to help them move about in the winter snow and in the marshy ground of summer. The feet of some lemmings change completely in winter to help them dig in the frozen ground.

Alistair Barnard

▲ *The third and fourth claws on the front feet of the collared lemming get much bigger each winter to help the lemming dig through frozen ground.*

◀ *The Arabian oryx lives in deserts where the temperatures are extreme. It copes with this harsh climate by feeding and moving about mainly at night, when it is cooler. Its white coat helps reflect the strong rays of the sun, and its splayed or slanting feet help it to walk on the sand. The temperature of its body changes — slowly rising during the day and falling below what is normal for mammals at night — to help it keep cool.*

Steve Kaufman/Bruce Coleman Ltd

# Why Mammals Do What They Do

The way mammals behave has a lot to do with the fact that all mammals, except for the monotremes, have babies that are born alive. These babies need to drink milk from their mothers in order to survive, and so it is important that a mammal mother cares about her young. Some mammals depend on their mothers for many months, or even years in the case of humans, apes, elephants, and whales.

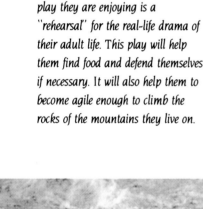

*▼ For these young chamois, the play they are enjoying is a "rehearsal" for the real-life drama of their adult life. This play will help them find food and defend themselves if necessary. It will also help them to become agile enough to climb the rocks of the mountains they live on.*

Gunter Ziesler/Bruce Coleman Ltd

### Looking after needs

Some mammal behavior has to do with the day-to-day things that individual mammals must do to look after their bodies. This behavior includes the way they feed, groom themselves, get rid of waste products such as urine and feces, and huddle together for warmth or safety.

### Relating to others

The first relationship that mammals have is with their mothers. This usually lasts only for a short time. For the rest of their lives, the way mammals behave with their group is very important to their survival.

### Playing

Play is a form of behavior found among some young mammals and not among others. Young humans, apes, monkeys, dogs, cats, weasels, and mongooses play a great deal. This play helps to develop the skills the young animals will need in the wild. Young carnivores, such as puppies and kittens, spend a lot of time pouncing on each other in mock attacks. Play among primates (monkeys, apes, and humans) helps them learn to relate to others in a group. They learn to read the signals sent by other individuals, such as if they feel tired, angry, happy, and so on.

### Leaders of the pack

Many mammals travel together in a group. Usually one animal is more important than the rest, but sometimes there may be a few dominant animals. In a troop of baboons the most powerful males travel in the middle of the group. You can pick them out easily

Purdy & Matthews/Planet Earth Pictures

because they are bigger than the rest and their manes are thicker.

Sometimes the color of the most important member is different from the others. The most important buck in a group of blackbucks is black, while all the other males are light brown. In some groups of monkeys, the most important male has a louder voice than the rest.

## Mating

Some mammals have many sexual partners during their lives. Others, such as some of the small, forest-living antelopes, mate for life. Some mammals, such as the Uganda kob antelope, court each other with a complicated display of actions and sounds. Others, such as the bandicoot, mate quickly and roughly and never see each other again.

Frieder Sauer/Bruce Coleman Ltd

▲ Many meat-eating mammals hunt together in order to fill their bellies. These female lions are responsible for finding food for their family group, or "pride." Together they can catch a much larger animal than they could if each was hunting alone. If they cannot catch their prey after a short dash, they will give up and try again later.

◄ These male impalas are rubbing heads as a sign of friendship. They exchange the scent made by the glands on their faces to show that they belong to the same group.

## Marking boundaries

Most mammals need to pass urine when their bladders become full. Cows, seals, whales, female dogs, and female mice, among others, urinate when a part of the brain is stimulated by a full bladder.

Adult male dogs, wolves, mice, and some other mammals do not pass urine only for this reason. A male sex hormone (testosterone) that is present in their bodies makes them behave in a different way. They leave urine at certain places around their homes so that other males will find it and keep away. They mark the boundaries of their territories by this behavior.

▲ Humans and tigers cannot live together side by side. In order for tigers to survive, large areas of forest must be set aside to provide enough food for these meat-eating mammals. By conserving the forest for the tigers, we are also conserving thousands of other types of animals and plants.

# Mammals in Danger

Ever since life began on Earth, certain groups of animals have died out or become extinct and been replaced with new groups. There is nothing new or unusual about this. But the rate at which species become extinct has skyrocketed in the last 30 years.

## Alarming extinctions

There are perhaps 10 million forms of life existing in the world today. Many more — mostly insects in places such as tropical rain forests — have probably not even been discovered yet. What zoologists do know is that there are about 4,300 species of mammal living now — that is all.

Between A.D. 1600 and 1900, a period of 300 years, about 75 species of birds and mammals became extinct. Another 75 disappeared between 1900 and the 1960s — the same number in a period of about 60 years. Since that time, the number of extinctions has skyrocketed.

Today 500 kinds of mammals are "at risk." This means that so many have been killed there is a chance that there won't be enough healthy adults left to breed and keep the species going. Some ecologists say that in the next quarter-century we can expect to lose at least 1,000 groups of plants and animals a year and as many as 100 types of plants and animals *each day*. This death rate is very alarming. By the year 2015, you will have witnessed the extinction of maybe a million living things.

## Humans are responsible

The number of humans is rapidly increasing, and we have become a big threat to all other forms of life on Earth. As the weapons we use have become more and more powerful and accurate, the danger to other creatures has increased. Once hunters used rocks and clubs, but now there are machine guns that can fire many shots very quickly. What chance do animals have against these killing machines?

It is important to realize that there are other ways of killing mammals than by shooting them. Humans now live in nearly all parts of the world. When we build towns and highways, animals lose their homes, food and water, and open space. Allowing too many sheep and cattle to graze on land turns it into desert where nothing will grow. Air and water pollution, acid rain, and soil contaminated by mining or the dumping of chemicals poison animals' homes and food. Oil spilled at sea sticks to marine mammals and many of them die. Logging kills the trees that are the food supply and home of many mammals.

We must learn to value the rest of the animal kingdom and realize that they have as much right to exist as we do.

# SOME OF THE SPECIES IN TROUBLE

## American bison

The American bison nearly became extinct a hundred years ago. Once, about 50 million of these animals covered the American prairies. The Indians who lived there depended on the bison, or "buffalo," as they became known, for their food and clothing. They had great respect for these enormous beasts.

Coo-ee Historical Picture Library

▲ When the Europeans arrived in America, there were about 50 million bison, but the "buffalo" hunters reduced them to fewer than 800 by 1884. Sometimes they would take only the tongue, which was a favorite food at the time.

▼ Today there are about 40,000 bison in the reserves that have been set aside for them.

Jeff Foott/ Bruce Coleman Ltd

## Sea songs

Did you know that whales can sing? The male humpback whale chirps, groans, and cries during the breeding season in a strange sort of underwater song. Female whales can hear these love songs up to 100 miles (160 km) away. Some of these songs have been recorded so humans can hear them too.

▼ *This 62-foot (19-m) humpback whale no longer has to fear the harpoon guns and factory ships that wiped out so many of its kind. Some species of whale, including the humpback, appear to be increasing in number.*

The arrival of the Europeans spelled trouble for the bison. Hunters killed millions of buffalo so that they could sell their meat and hides. Buffalo Bill counted 4,280 animals that he killed in one year all by himself. By 1884 bison had almost disappeared.

At the last moment, reserves were set aside for them. Now, there are thousands of bison in reserves such as Yellowstone and Wood Buffalo national parks. But the huge herds will never thunder across the plains again.

## Humpback whale

People have hunted whales for many hundreds of years for the money to be made by selling their meat, oil, and bones. Humpbacks are one of the easiest sorts of whales to catch. As long as the whalers had small boats and had to kill the huge mammals by hand, the whales at least had a chance. But when huge factory ships appeared, the whales were in very bad trouble.

These huge ships carry helicopters, explosive harpoon guns, and sonar to detect a whale's exact position in the sea. The processing of the whale meat and other parts of their bodies takes place on board the ship.

After many attempts by concerned scientists and the general public, an international ban on commercial whaling became law in 1986. This is the first time in the history of humans that these creatures have been protected.

## Mountain gorilla

Humans are the worst enemies of Africa's gorillas. Poachers sell their heads and hands to tourists as souvenirs. A woman named Dian Fossey lived in Africa for almost 20 years, studying the mountain gorillas. Dr. Fossey became friends with several groups of them and wrote a book called *Gorillas in the Mist* to make the world aware of their plight. The book

was later made into a movie.

Although African laws now say that you are not allowed to kill these animals, it is very hard to make sure that everyone obeys. Even in the park that has been set aside for them, the gorillas are not entirely safe. Loggers cut the trees they feed on and hunters are still killing them. There are only 350 to 500 mountain gorillas left. Some people feel that the best way to protect them is by encouraging tourists to visit them. This way these gentle mammals will be protected, and the people who live nearby will earn money they badly need from the tourist business.

## Maned wolf

Maned wolves live on the dry, grassy plains of some South American countries. They look like red dogs on stilts, and although they are as big as wolves and are called wolves, they are really a type of fox. Maned wolves can travel distances of 20 miles (30 km) a night, and they hunt rabbits, rats, mice, and other rodents, as well as birds.

These mammals are hunted by collectors for zoos as well as by the local people, who use parts of the body for medicine and the left eye to make lucky charms. Because of these problems and the diseases they suffer from, there are only about 2,000 maned wolves alive today.

▲ *This gentle giant looks very wise as it stares out at the world from the safety of its mountain home. Let us hope that the people who live near the gorillas in Africa are encouraged to protect them from logging and poaching.*

◀ *The maned wolf of South America has matching black "stockings" on its legs and a black "cape" over its shoulders. There are so few of these animals left that they will probably not be able to survive in the wild.*

# Kangaroos and Wallabies

Kangaroos are probably the most recent group of marsupials to appear. There are more than 50 types of kangaroos, tree-kangaroos, and wallabies. A wallaby is a small species of kangaroo.

Most kangaroos live in Australia, but tree-kangaroos and wallabies are also found in New Guinea. Kangaroos and wallabies have short front legs and large, strong back legs with long back feet. When they need to move fast they hop on their back legs, using their long tails to help them balance. The strong tail acts as a fifth limb when the animal is moving slowly.

Tree-kangaroos have very long, strong front legs and shortened, wide back feet. They can walk along a flat branch or climb upward by gripping with the claws

Jean-Paul Ferrero/Auscape International

## I know you can hop, but can you walk?

Kangaroos probably started off by bounding rather than hopping. In time, their back legs grew longer and so did their back feet. When they are moving at the same speed, a hopping kangaroo uses up less energy than a running dog or a galloping horse. This is good for the kangaroo in one way, but the design of its back legs means that a kangaroo cannot walk at all. Neither can it move each back leg by itself unless the animal is swimming.

◄ *This hopping kangaroo is moving along very fast. Kangaroos can hop at 30 miles per hour (48 kilometers per hour), but only for short distances.*

David Kirshner

▲ This Goodfellow's tree-kangaroo is the most brightly colored of all the tree-kangaroos. Long ago it probably lived on the ground, but now it has adapted to living in trees, which is why it looks different from its ground-living relatives.

David Kirshner

of all four feet.

All kangaroos are herbivores (plant-eaters). Some types snatch at plants as they move from place to place, while others stay in one spot and graze like cattle and sheep.

## Taking care of joey

Female kangaroos have a deep pouch that opens forward, not backward like most other marsupials. A newborn baby has to climb up to the opening and then tumble down inside to find a teat to drink from. Although kangaroos have four teats, they have only one baby at a time. The baby is called a joey.

The joeys are very small when they are born — a female red kangaroo can weigh 60 pounds (27 kg) yet give birth to a joey that weighs only $\frac{1}{30}$ ounce (800 mg)! A joey that is 1 month old is still blind and has no hair, although it does have its back legs and its tail. Long after it is able to move about by itself, the young kangaroo goes back to its mother's pouch to sleep, travel, and avoid danger.

▲ This red kangaroo is the largest of all living marsupials. Elderly males can be as tall as 8 feet (2 m) when they are sitting down and much more when they are propped up by the tail. The females are smaller and not even red, but a bluish-gray color, as are about a third of the males.

# Orangutans

The word "orangutan" means "wild person" or "man of the woods." These large apes are found in the wild in only two places in the world — Borneo and the northern part of Sumatra (two large islands between the continents of Asia and Australia).

▼ This large adult male comes from the island of Sumatra. He has large, flat cheek flanges and a long, red beard and moustache.

John Cancalosi/ Bruce Coleman Ltd

Orangutans are covered with rather uneven clumps of red hair — you can see their rough, blue-gray skin underneath. Their arms are so long that their legs look short in comparison.

Their hands and feet are powerful and curved. The orangs found on Borneo look a bit different from the ones that live on Sumatra.

The females stop growing at about 7 years old, when they weigh 73 to 92 pounds (33 to 42 kg) and stand 42 to 47 inches (107 to 120 cm) tall. Males keep growing until they are 13 to 15 years old. A fully grown male weighs 176 to 200 pounds (80 to 91 kg) and measures 53 to 55 inches (136 to 141 cm) tall.

## Looking for a partner

These red apes spend most of their lives alone. Both males and females wander about during the day looking for food. The males travel farther distances than the females. When a female is ready to mate, she searches for a male partner. Male orangs signal their whereabouts by making a series of deep roars that can be heard from quite a long way off. This roaring keeps away other males but attracts the females nearby. A mating couple stays together for a few days and then the two go their separate ways. The gestation period for orangs is 245 days.

## A diet of fruit and leaves

Orangs eat a lot of fruit — it makes up more than half their diet. They also eat leaves, bark, and insects when they can get them. Because the trees of their rain forest home do not produce fruit in any particular season, it is important that these large mammals remember where their favorite fruiting trees are so that they can find them again easily.

## Will they survive in the wild?

Mother orangutans used to be shot and their babies collected for zoos. This practice has been stopped, and orangutans are now protected. The main threat to them is the destruction of the forests they live in. Orangutans do breed well in zoos, and their number in captivity is growing.

▲ *The orangutan, or "man of the woods," looks less like a human than many of the other large apes. But don't be deceived, because orangs are very intelligent.*

## Sleeping close to the stars

At night each orangutan builds its own nest in a tree. Leaves and twigs are packed into the top branches of the tree to make a platform. When the animal lies down, it pulls more vegetation over itself like a blanket. Sometimes a nest is used again, but usually a new one is made every night.

▶ *This orang is looking down on the world from the safety of its nest in a treetop. Orangs are such large animals that only one adult fits in each nest.*

▼ *What has this young mountain gorilla just discovered about its mother? Babies like this one make up 40 percent of the mountain gorilla population. The gestation period for gorillas is 267 days.*

# Gorillas and Chimpanzees

*T*he gorilla is the world's largest living primate (the group of mammals that includes humans, apes, and monkeys). Gorillas live in several areas of Africa. Chimpanzees can be found in West, East, and Central Africa. They live in many different types of forest areas.

## Gorillas

An adult male gorilla weighs 385 pounds (175 kg) and is about 61 inches (156 cm) tall when he stands up on two legs. The female is much smaller. She weighs 187 pounds (85 kg) and stands 54 inches (137 cm) tall. When a male is fully grown, he grows a silvery-white "saddle" across his back that contrasts with the rest of his black hair. This is why adult males are known as silverbacks.

## Ground-dwelling troops

A gorilla troop is made up of a silverback male (sometimes there are more than one), a few males that are not fully grown, several females, and the young ones. They live mainly on the ground. Even the nests they build at night are usually on the ground. Gorillas do climb, but they don't do so very often. When they travel long distances, they go on all four legs with their hands placed so that their weight rests on the

Yann Arthus-Bertrand / Auscape International

middle joints of the fingers. This is called knuckle-walking. Gorillas in mountain areas feed on bamboo shoots, tall herbs, and small trees. In the lowland areas they eat more fruit, especially tough, woody fruits.

## Gorillas in captivity

Gorillas kept in zoos and research centers are able to learn many things. They form close relationships with their trainers and sometimes with other animals and can learn sign language to communicate with humans.

## Chimpanzees

The chimpanzee has black hair, smooth black skin, and uses its knuckles to walk, as the gorilla does. The common male weighs 130 pounds (60 kg) and is about 47 inches (120 cm) tall when it stands on two feet. The common female weighs about 105 pounds (47.5 kg) and is nearly as tall as the male.

Chimpanzees spend about half their time on the ground, but they can climb very well. At night they make their nests in the trees, as the orangutans do. These nests are not made as well as the orangs' platforms are, though. Some-times, when it is hot, they build nests for naps in the middle of the day. Gorillas do this too.

Fruit is the most important part of a chimpanzee's diet. But these animals also feed on leaves, bark, insects, and middle-size mammals such as monkeys. The males do most of the hunting.

## Living in groups

Chimpanzees live in large groups that some scientists call communities and others call unit-groups. There are from 20 to 100 animals living in a group. A community lives in its own territory with boundaries that are patrolled by the adult males to keep out strangers. Adult males seem to stay in the communities in which they were born, but females seem to join other ones nearby.

A female that is ready to mate may do so with a large number of the males hanging around her. Or, she may choose

The Gorilla Foundation/National Geographic Society

one male and go off with him for several days. The gestation period for chimpanzees is 230 days. A mother will nurse her baby for 2 to 3 years, or even longer. She has her babies 4 years apart, so she has plenty of time to do this.

## Almost human

Chimpanzees are very intelligent animals and can learn to do all sorts of difficult things. They can learn to use tools and to work machines. You can also teach them to use signs with their hands to communicate with humans, as you can with gorillas.

▲ *Koko, a female gorilla, is playing with her pet kitten, All Ball. Koko loved the kitten and was very sad when it was killed by a car. Now she has a new feline friend.*

▼ *This young chimpanzee is using a stick as a tool to get grubs out of rotten wood.*

Peter Davey/Bruce Coleman Ltd

# Bears and Pandas

The ancestors of our modern bears had long tails and were fairly small. Over the years, bears have grown bigger. Now they are the biggest of all the carnivores (meat-eaters) that live on the land. Male polar bears may weigh more than 1,750 pounds (800 kg).

Bears have huge heads, thick strong bodies, and short tails (except for the red panda). They have the largest molars (teeth suited for grinding) of all the meat-eating mammals.

Most bears have fur that is all one color. The only ones that do not are the giant panda and the red panda. Nearly all marking of a different color is found on the chest.

The members of the bear family live on the land. The only one that does not is the polar bear, which lives partly in the water. Three types sleep during the day and come out at night. These are the red panda, the sloth bear, and the sun bear. All the rest are active during the day and sleep at night.

In the winter there is no food for the bears that live in the northern parts of the world. They have to store up fat in their bodies and then find a den or cave in which to hibernate for the long winter months. During these months they do not eat but live off their body fat.

It is during these cozy winter months that the mother gives birth to between 1 and 5 very small young ones, called cubs. They are protected all the time by their mother.

## Polar bears

Polar bears live in the harsh Arctic environment. They feed on mammals, such as seals, that live in the sea. Polar bears often float on ice for 40 to 50 miles (65 to 80 km) to look for seals.

▼ *Most bears have a similar body shape, as you can tell from these drawings. Despite their ferocious image, bears eat mostly plants and insects, but like all carnivores they will not turn down a good piece of meat when they see it.*

Sun bear

Sloth bear

Brown bear

Polar bear

Himalayan black bear

Dorothy Dunphy

David Kirshner

◀ *The red panda weighs only 6½ to 11 pounds (3 to 5 kg). It eats bamboo, other plants, and even insects.*

Female polar bears do not have babies until they are 5 years old. When they are pregnant, they go away by themselves to a den to have their young.

## Brown and black bears

The brown bear is also known as the grizzly bear and Kodiak bear in North America and the Kamchatkan bear in Asia. Along with the Asian black bear and the American black bear, it feeds on roots, berries, fish, and dead meat.

## Pandas

The giant panda and the red panda are the only carnivores that feed almost entirely on bamboo. Although these two animals do not look alike, they are both called pandas because they have adapted in similar ways to feed on bamboo. Both species of panda are found in China, and the red panda also lives in Nepal.

The giant panda has a large wrist bone that acts like a thumb for grasping bamboo. The red panda has a much smaller version of this.

▼ *This giant panda relaxes against a rock to enjoy its meal. Giant pandas eat only bamboo.*

Spectacled bear

American black bear

Philippa Scott/NHPA

A. Visage/Auscape International

▲ *Most tigers live in hot, wet countries near the equator. But these tigers live in Siberia, one of the coldest and loneliest places in the world. Their home is covered in deep snow during the winter months — you can see some of it sprinkled over their backs.*

# Great Cats

**O**f all the carnivorous (meat-eating) mammals, the cat family eats the most meat. Most cats eat nothing but red meat, but some cats enjoy other foods as well. The fishing cat, for example, enjoys snakes, snails, and fish, and the flat-headed cat eats fruit.

## Roars and purrs

One difference between big cats and small cats, apart from size, is that the small cats can purr but don't seem to be able to roar very well, and the big cats can roar but not purr. If your pet cat starts to make very deep roaring noises, watch out!

## Cheetahs

Cheetahs have smallish, black spots marking their fur. They weigh from 77 to 143 pounds (35 to 65 kg). Their bodies are not as heavy as those of lions and tigers because they are the athletes of the cat family: they can run faster than any other living creature. Cheetahs have been clocked at more than 60 mph (100 km/h).

Cheetahs run using short bursts of speed, but they use so much energy during these bursts that they get very hot. They must stop after about 20 seconds or they become short of breath. So if a cheetah doesn't catch the prey it is chasing during this time, it may lose it. Cheetahs can be found on the African plains.

## Tigers

Tigers are the largest members of the cat family. They are known to add humans to their diet when there isn't enough to eat, but they prefer other prey. Troublesome tigers are usually tracked down and killed or sent to zoos.

Tigers have black stripes running across their backs. They are large, heavy animals; tigers weigh from 280 to 660 pounds (130 to 300 kg). The animals they hunt are large too.

Tigers tend to be loners. If they aren't

by themselves, the most likely group you'll see together is a mother and her young cubs. These large mammals hunt by themselves and will stay hidden waiting to ambush their prey rather than chasing it the way cheetahs do.

## Lions

Most lions live in Africa, but a small number of lions still exist in India. Lions like company — no living alone for them. The group they live in is called a pride. Each pride has 5 to 15 adult females and their cubs and 1 to 6 adult males. The males usually leave the pride at some stage.

Lions hunt together. The adult females spread out and surround their prey. They slowly stalk their chosen animal until they are ready to pounce.

There is more difference in appearance between male and female lions than between the males and females of other large cats. The male lion's head is crowned by a huge, shaggy mane, but females don't have a mane at all. The males are much larger than the females. Lions weigh from 260 to 520 pounds (120 to 240 kg).

## Leopards and jaguars

Leopards are found in Africa and Asia. Jaguars are found in Central and South America and always live near water.

Some leopards have large, black spots on their bodies; others are all black and often live in tropical forests. Snow leopards have big paws that help them to walk in the snow. Some jaguars are large and spotted; others are black.

Most leopards weigh between 65 and 155 pounds (30 and 70 kg). Jaguars usually weigh between 80 and 120 pounds (36 and 55 kg). Some huge jaguars from Brazil weigh up to 300 pounds (136 kg).

These cats hunt alone. The animals they choose as prey are smaller than those hunted by lions and tigers. Leopards are very good at climbing trees and often wedge their prey into the fork of a tree to keep it safe. The clouded leopard hunts animals that live on the ground or in trees, such as pigs, monkeys, and birds. Snow leopards hunt mostly medium-size mammals with hooves, such as antelopes.

Jonathan Scott/Planet Earth Pictures

▲ *Can you tell which is the male lion and which is the female?*

Anup & Manoj Shah/Planet Earth Pictures

◀ *The cheetah is famous as a sprinter rather than as a long-distance runner. Look how sleek and lithe this fastest of all animals is.*

# Seals, Sea Lions, and Walruses

S eals, sea lions, fur seals, and walruses are all pinnipeds — a word derived from Latin roots meaning "winged feet." Pinnipeds have streamlined bodies, a thick layer of fat (blubber) under their skin to keep them warm, very short legs, and "hands" and "feet" modified into flippers. Flippers are like a human hand with all the fingers inside a mitten.

▼ This is a big, crowded colony of male, female, and pup California sea lions. These are probably the noisiest seals, barking almost continuously. Their small external ear pinna can be seen.

Frans Lanting/Bruce Coleman Ltd

Pinnipeds spend much of their lives at sea, catching fish and squid on which they feed, but return to land once a year to have their pups. Sharks, killer whales, and polar bears are their main enemies.

There are three main groups of pinnipeds. Sea lions and fur seals have a very small external ear pinna and can bend their hind flippers forward at the ankle. True seals have no external pinna and cannot bend their hind flippers forward, so they have some difficulty moving on land. Walruses have no pinna but can bend their hind flippers forward. The external pinna is the fleshy ear flap that most mammals have. In sea lions and fur seals it is narrow and about 2½ inches (6 cm) long. Pinnipeds can hear well in air and particularly well in water.

## Sea lions

The five species of sea lion live mostly along the shores of the Pacific, but one is found only in Australia and another on the Auckland Islands south of New Zealand. The California sea lion is often seen performing in zoos and circuses.

All sea lions are big animals, the males ranging from 6 to 10 feet (2 to 3 m) long, with a dark brown coat and a longer, rougher mane on the neck. The females are slightly smaller and lighter in color than males.

## Fur seals

There are nine species of fur seal. The northern fur seal has its headquarters on the Pribilof Islands in the Bering Sea. When these islands were discovered in 1786, fur seals were very numerous and were killed for their soft fur coats. As the seal numbers became reduced, it was necessary for the North Pacific nations to agree to look after the herd. Only a certain number and size of young males are allowed to be taken during the month of June. As there are many surplus males in the herd, this agreement has allowed the herd to build up again, and the population has recovered.

The eight species of southern fur seal are found mostly in the Southern Hemisphere, on the shores of Australia, New Zealand, South Africa, South America, and on many of the sub-Antarctic islands. When early navigators were exploring the world, they killed large numbers of these seals for their coats, and the seals were nearly exterminated. Many populations are still low, but others are increasing.

All fur seals are similar in color — males are dark blackish brown with rough manes; females are lighter. Adult males, depending on the species, range from 5 to 7 feet (1.5 to 2.2 m) in length. Newborn pups are 24 to 32 inches (60 to 80 cm) long and have a soft, black coat, shed when they are about 3 months old.

▲ *Cape fur seals live on the southern coasts of both South Africa and Australia. There are many black-coated pups in this picture, also big bulls and smaller females. You can see the small external ear pinna and the way the hind flippers can bend forward at the ankles.*

▶ A *big herd of walruses is hauled out on a rocky beach on an Arctic island. On a sunny day like this, more blood goes through the blood vessels in the skin so the walrus doesn't get too hot, and the skin looks pinker.*

Leonard Lee Rue III/Bruce Coleman Ltd

## Pinniped words

These are some of the words you will meet when reading about pinnipeds:

**herd**: a large group

**rookery**: a breeding group

**bull**: an adult male

**bachelor**: a male that is not fully mature

**cow**: a female

**pup**: a young seal from birth to about 4 months

**calf**: a young walrus from birth to about 4 months

**yearling**: young between about 4 months and 1 year old

**pod**: a group of pups

**seal**: a general term used for sea lions, fur seals, or true seals

## Walruses

Walruses live in the shallower waters of the Arctic seas and are often found in large herds on moving pack ice. Walruses are the second largest of the pinnipeds. Adult males may be 10 feet (3 m) long and weigh 2,600 pounds (1.2 tonnes). The skin is rough and wrinkled, with few hairs.

The conspicuous long upper tusks, present in both males and females, may be 3 feet (1 m) long, though about 14 inches (35 cm) is usual. The ivory of these tusks has long been used for carvings; beautiful chess pieces were carved from them 800 years ago. Walruses use their tusks and strong whiskers to stir up the muddy sea bottom to find clams and cockles, which they suck out of the shells.

## True seals

In the Northern Hemisphere live ten different species of true seal. Each species has its preferred locality — near the North Pole, near Greenland, the Arctic coast of Russia, in the North Pacific and North Atlantic, around the shores of the British Isles and

Scandinavia, and in the Caspian Sea and Lake Baikal.

They vary in size (4 to 6 feet/1.3 to 1.8 m) and in color but are usually grayish with darker spots, splashes, or rings. The male harp seal has a harp, or horseshoe-shaped, dark pattern on its back, while the strikingly marked ribbon seal is dark brown with wide white bands around the neck, hind end, and each front flipper. The pups of many of these northern seals are born with a white woolly coat, shed for an adult coat at about 3 weeks.

Almost all the southern true seals live in the Southern Hemisphere. The main exceptions are the rare monk seals of the Hawaiian Islands and the Mediterranean Sea. The four Antarctic seals are the Weddell, crabeater, Ross, and leopard seals. The Weddell seal lives farthest south, close to the Antarctic continent. The very abundant crabeater seal does not eat crabs, but shrimp-like krill, which it sieves from the water through the spaces in its complicated teeth. Ross seals are relatively uncommon but are fast swimmers that catch squid and octopus. The leopard seal is fairly solitary and may range as far north as Australia.

Elephant seals are the largest of the pinnipeds. Adult males reach 13 to 16 feet (4 to 5 m) in length and weigh 7,940 pounds (3.6 tonnes). The elongated proboscis of the male hangs down over the mouth and gives the animal its name. One species lives on most of the sub-Antarctic islands and the other species on islands off the California coast. Elephant seals were once hunted for their blubber but are now protected.

Norman R. Lightfoot/Bruce Coleman Ltd

## How pinnipeds give birth

Most seals have a gestation period of about 11 months and produce a single pup, usually in spring or summer. The pups suckle on milk from their mothers, some for nearly a year, some for 3 or 4 months, and some for as little as 12 days, depending on the species of seal. The milk is very rich — 50 percent fat, compared with 3.5 percent fat in cow's milk. In this way the pup grows fast and puts on a thick layer of blubber. Walruses have a longer gestation period of 15 months, so the females can produce only 1 calf every 2 years. Some seals gather in big herds to have their pups; others stay in small family groups. There is much variation, according to the species of seal.

## Champion divers

All seals can stay underwater for a long time. The champion diver is the southern elephant seal, which can dive to 4,000 feet (1,200 m) and stay under for nearly 2 hours, although 20 to 30 minutes is much more usual. How do they manage to do this? Seals have a lot of blood in their bodies, much more than a human of similar size, and this blood carries a lot of oxygen. When a seal dives, the arteries in the less important parts of the body constrict, so hardly any blood gets through. In this way most of the blood with its oxygen goes to the brain. The heart rate slows down so the blood pressure remains normal.

▲ *This is a male hooded seal from the Arctic. Its nose area can be inflated to form a cushion — or "hood" — on top of the head. It can also close one nostril and blow out the soft membrane between the two sides of the nose to form a red "balloon." This looks spectacular, but we do not know why it is done.*

Bruce Coleman Ltd

◄ *A female harp seal lies on the Arctic ice next to her white-coated pup. Her hind flippers are held backward, and you can see the five digits, which have a membrane of skin between them so the flipper can be used for swimming.*

# Whales and Dolphins

Whales and dolphins are found in all the seas of the world and in some rivers and lakes. This group of mammals is divided into two smaller groups — the baleen (or whalebone) whales and the toothed whales.

## Baleen whales

There are three families of baleen, or whalebone, whales. These are right whales, gray whales, and rorquals. They are found in all oceans, and they migrate from one ocean to another at different times of the year.

Baleen whales have a mesh of bone in their mouths instead of normal teeth. This elastic, horny substance grows in the upper jaw and is known as whalebone, or baleen. The mesh acts as a sieve and lets the whales strain very small sea creatures called plankton out of the water. The type of plankton whales eat depends on where they are living at the time.

## Toothed whales

There are six families of toothed whales. They are sperm whales, white whales, beaked whales, dolphins, porpoises, and river dolphins. Toothed whales live in all kinds of water. Some types of dolphin are found only in rivers, some only in the parts of the ocean closest to land, while others live only in the open sea, far from land. On the other hand, the killer whale and the bottlenose dolphin live both close to land and in the deepest parts of the ocean.

Toothed whales have teeth that are shaped like cones. The teeth are designed to seize and hold prey; they are no good for chewing. Some toothed

▼ These drawings of the skeletons of baleen and toothed whales show the differences between them. You can see that the baleen whale has no teeth and the toothed whale does. Have a close look and see what other differences you can find. One thing you can't see in this drawing is the difference in size between the two. Baleen whales are much longer than toothed whales.

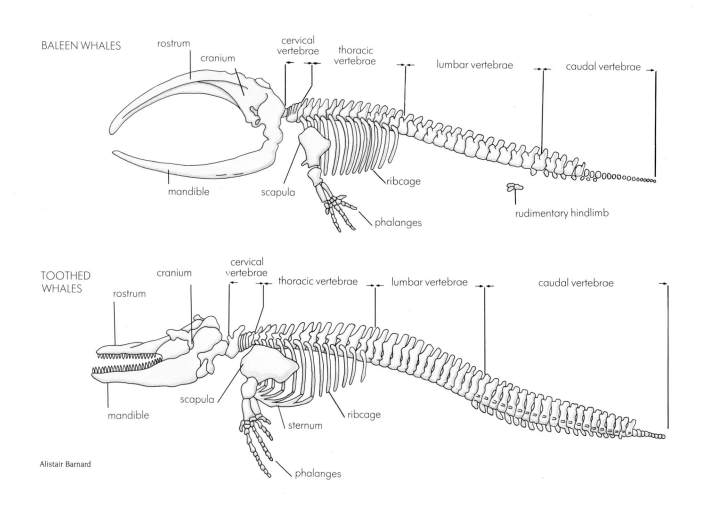

BALEEN WHALES — rostrum, cranium, cervical vertebrae, thoracic vertebrae, lumbar vertebrae, caudal vertebrae, mandible, scapula, ribcage, phalanges, rudimentary hindlimb

TOOTHED WHALES — rostrum, cranium, cervical vertebrae, thoracic vertebrae, lumbar vertebrae, caudal vertebrae, mandible, scapula, sternum, ribcage, phalanges

Alistair Barnard

D. Parer & E. Parer-Cook/Auscape International

◀ *Killer whales work together to herd prey into shallow water, where they can catch them. These whales eat seals and penguins as well as large fishes.*

## From the smallest to the largest

The smallest member of the order of whales and dolphins is Heaviside's dolphin. It is 4 feet (1.2 m) long and weighs 88 pounds (40 kg).

The largest member is the blue whale. It can grow up to 100 feet (30 m) long and weigh up to 286,500 pounds (130 tonnes).

## Did you know?

These whales and dolphins are listed as being in danger of dying out: the Chinese river dolphin, Indus dolphin, blue whale, humpback whale, black right whale, and the bowhead whale. Wouldn't it be a shame if these mammals disappeared altogether?

Nowadays whales are protected. Only nations that wish to study them for scientific reasons are allowed to catch them. There are new problems, though. Each year countless dolphins drown in the huge nets that some fishermen use to catch fish in the ocean. River dolphins are dying out because of water pollution and the fact that more and more boats are using the rivers.

Francisco Erize/Bruce Coleman Ltd

▲ *These bottle-nose dolphins are leaping, or breaching, to help them move faster through the water. You may have seen this kind of dolphin performing leaps at aquariums and zoos. Although dolphins have large brains, they are no smarter than many other mammals.*

whales, such as the common dolphin, have more than a hundred teeth in each jaw, while others, such as Risso's dolphin, have only six to eight teeth in the lower jaw.

Most toothed whales feed on fish, squid, and octopus. But the killer whale also eats the meat of warm-blooded animals such as seals, sea lions, dolphins, and penguins.

## Shaped like a torpedo for life in the sea

The torpedo-shaped bodies of whales and dolphins are perfect for moving through the water. The front flippers act as stiff paddles that help these creatures to steer and keep their balance.

Their skin is smooth and has practically no hair. They do not have ears on the outside of their bodies. Under their skin is a layer of blubber (whale fat), which keeps them warm no matter what the temperature is outside.

Whales vary in color from white to all black, with different shades of gray in between. Many types are dark gray or black on their backs and the top of their heads, and light gray or white underneath. One of the most interesting-looking whales is the killer whale, which has black and white markings.

Most whales and their relatives have a single baby at a time. It is rare for them to have twins. The gestation period for a whale is 11 to 16 months, depending on what type it is. The new baby, called a calf, is about one-third the size of its mother when it is born. The calf sucks from its mother's teats and grows very quickly because the milk it drinks is very rich and full of protein.

Francois Gohier/Ardea London

## Thar she blows!

Human beings can't stay underwater for very long without breathing aids such as aqualungs. But whales don't need to breathe as often as land mammals. They can hold their breath for a very long time when they are diving. Their lungs don't hold more air than land mammals of the same size, but they take larger breaths and get more oxygen from the air they breathe.

Instead of having nostrils, whales have a blowhole. This blowhole closes over when the whale is underwater and opens when it comes to the surface. When the whale surfaces, it breathes out, and you can see a spout, or "blow." The spout is made up of moist air, a fine mist of water, small droplets of oil, and mucus.

◀ *This blue whale is "blowing" now that it has come to the surface of the water. Baleen whales like this one have two blowholes. Toothed whales have a single blowhole.*

# Why do live whales get stranded on beaches?

Whales seem to be able to receive information from the Earth's magnetic field about where they are and where they should be going. Imagine that the Earth is like a magnet and has areas of force around it that carry electric current. Whales can sense these areas of force, which are affected by the eruptions of underwater volcanoes, the shift in the position of the continents, and so on. They use this information to navigate or steer by, in the same way that the captain of a ship uses a compass.

But sometimes, it seems, whales make mistakes with the information they receive, and whole groups of them become stranded on the shore.

▲ *This huge humpback whale looks like a torpedo as it leaps out of the water. It weighs about 110,000 pounds (50 tonnes). One of the largest of the filter-feeding whales, it eats very small fish that swim together in schools, as well as tiny shrimp-like creatures called krill.*

▶ *These sperm whales became confused in shallow water and were stranded at low tide on a beach in southeastern Australia. Sometimes people manage to keep beached whales alive until the next high tide and float them so that they can swim away. At other times the whales are not so lucky and die.*

# Sea Cows

Sea cows probably have the same ancient ancestor as elephants. There have never been many different types of sea cows, and only four types survive today — one species of dugong and three species of manatee. They may look the same, but there are differences.

## Underwater grazers

These large mammals are called sea cows because they graze on plants and grasses the way cows do. The difference is, of course, that what they feed on are water plants and sea grasses. Because some of these underwater plants have a substance like sand in them, the teeth of sea cows become damaged when they chew them. Manatees overcome this problem by replacing their teeth when the old ones wear out. The old front teeth drop out, and new teeth come through at the back of the jaw. The dugongs have two back teeth that keep growing all through their lives, so they never get worn away.

Another difference between dugongs and manatees is that dugongs have a snout (nose) that points downward, so these mammals have to eat plants that grow on the bottom of the ocean. The manatees do not have a snout at such an angle, so they can also eat plants living at or near the surface of the water.

Dugongs live only in the sea, while manatees also live in the mouths of rivers and in the rivers themselves. This means that manatees can live in fresh water as well as salt water.

Manatees are larger than dugongs. They measure 8 to 14 feet (2.5 to 4.5 m) from head to tail and weigh 770 to 3,300 pounds (350 to 1,500 kg). Dugongs measure up to 10 feet (3 m) from head to tail and weigh 880 to 1,110 pounds (400 to 500 kg).

## A tale of two tails

Although dugongs and manatees look fairly similar, their tails make it easy to tell them apart. Dugongs have triangular-shaped tails like those of whales and dolphins. Manatees have flat tails shaped like a paddle, rather like those of beavers or platypuses.

## Good mothers

Female dugongs and manatees look after their babies very well. They communicate with their calves by chirping like birds and by making high-pitched squeaks and squeals. A young calf stays close to its mother and often rides on her back. Although a calf starts eating plants soon after it is born, it drinks from its mother until it is about 18 months old. The breasts of these mammals are found near the bottom of their flippers. They look rather like a

▼ Manatees like these are found in both seas and rivers. They eat sea grasses as well as plants floating on top of the water. You can see that their noses are fairly flat, which allows them to feed this way.

female human's breasts, and some people think this is what started the legends about mermaids — those imaginary sea creatures that look like a woman from the waist up and a fish from the waist down.

## Doomed because they're delicious?

Unfortunately for them, the meat of dugongs and manatees tastes very good. Many people, such as some Australian Aborigines, say it is their favorite food. It does not taste like fish but more like veal, beef, or pork. This is because, like the land mammals we use for meat, sea cows feed on plants. Because of hunting, and because of polluted water, the numbers of these gentle mammals began to decrease. Today, even though they are such a good source of food, most sea cows are protected. If their feeding grounds are preserved, perhaps their numbers will begin to increase.

▲ *If you look closely at this female dugong and her baby, you can see the way their snouts point downward and the way their tails have two triangular halves, or flukes, just like whales. Females are at least 10 years old before they have their first calf, and then they feed them for up to 18 months.*

# Elephants

The ancestors of elephants are thought to have lived 50 to 60 million years ago. Once there were many different species, including the woolly mammoth. Nowadays, there are only two species left — African elephants and Asian elephants.

Joanna Van Gruisen/Ardea London

▲ *This mother Asian elephant and her baby live on the island of Sri Lanka. You can see that she does not have visible tusks and that her back is humped. Her calf fits nicely under her belly.*

## African elephants

African elephants have very large ears — much larger than those of Asian elephants. These act as radiators to get rid of unwanted heat from an elephant's body. African elephants are heavier and taller than Asian elephants. A male (bull) elephant can weigh more than 14,000 pounds (7 tonnes) and can stand more than 12 feet (4 m) tall.

African elephants have a back that is curved downward (concave). Males and females both have tusks. The trunks of African elephants have more folds, or rings, than those of Asian elephants and seem quite floppy. At the end of the trunk there are two finger-like parts sticking out.

## Asian elephants

Asian elephants have smaller ears and smaller, lighter bodies than their African relatives. The heaviest Asian elephant that we know of weighed 12,000 pounds (5.4 tonnes) and was about 11 feet (3.3 m) tall.

Asian elephants have a humped (convex) or flat back. The females do not usually have tusks. The trunks of Asians seem to be stiffer than those of African

▶ *This baby African elephant has very big ears, doesn't it? Elephants raise and flap their ears when they are alarmed, angry, excited, or want to keep cool.*

D. Parer & E. Parer-Cook/Auscape International

## An elephant beauty treatment — mud, mud, and more mud

Wallowing in mud seems to be an important part of everyday elephant behavior. The mud protects the elephant's sensitive skin against the strong rays of the sun, against insect bites, and against loss of moisture. So just remember, elephants were the first ones to use the mud bath as a beauty treatment.

▲ *These African elephants are wallowing in thick, gray mud that matches their gray bodies. The layer of mud that dries on their skin protects them from insect bites and sunburn. Elephants that wallow in water toss dust on their backs to get a similar sort of protection.*

elephants. The top part of the end of the trunk sticks out like a finger.

### An elephant's skin

An elephant has very thick skin on most parts of its body, especially around the back and on some parts of the head. Even though the skin is so thick, it is sensitive because there are many nerve endings in it.

Most elephants have gray bodies, but African elephants often look brown or even red. This is because they wallow in mudholes or plaster colored soil on their skin. The mud protects the elephant's sensitive skin.

### Elephant babies

Female elephants usually have 1 baby (called a calf) at a time. A newborn calf weighs 170 to 300 pounds (77 to 136 kg) and measures 3 feet (91 cm) at the shoulder. The babies are quite hairy compared with their parents, but they lose much of this hair as they get older. Calves can drink up to 3 gallons (11.4 l) of milk a day. Some continue nursing until they are 10 years old.

45

A female elephant that lives for 50 to 70 years could have 7 or 8 babies during her life, but very few have this many.

## What elephants eat and how they behave

The African elephant feeds mostly on branches, twigs, and leaves; the Asian elephant feeds mostly on grasses. During a drought the oldest female elephant (called the matriarch) will lead her family and relatives to the best places to find food. The rest of the herd learn her secrets and in turn pass on important information about how to

◄ *African elephants feed on the leaves and branches of trees. One of their favorite trees is the acacia. When it is hard to find food, they push over trees to reach the twigs at the top. Asian elephants prefer grasses and shrubs.*

## 1,001 uses for a trunk

The trunk of an elephant is a very important part of its body. It is really the animal's nose and upper lip joined together. The first scientists to write about nature (naturalists) described it as "the elephant's hand" or "the snake hand."

The things an elephant can do with its trunk are extraordinary. It is able to pick up something as small as a coin. A 25-year-old female Asian elephant was seen cracking peanuts with the back of her trunk, blowing the shells away, and eating the nut inside.

An elephant's trunk does not have any bones in it. It is made up of more than 100,000 different muscle parts, plus blood vessels, nerves, some fat, tissue to hold it together, skin, hair, and bristles. The nostrils continue as separate openings from one end of the trunk to the other.

The trunk of an adult Asian elephant can hold 2.2 gallons (8.5 l) of water. A thirsty adult bull (male) elephant can drink 56 gallons (212 l) in just under 5 minutes.

Trunks are used for all sorts of things —

feeding, watering, dusting, smelling, touching, lifting, communicating with other animals, and as a weapon for protecting and defending the elephant or any young ones in danger.

▲ *These African elephants are touching each other as elephant friends do. Behavior like this is important among members of a herd as part of their social activity.*

# Killed for their tusks

Tusks are very useful to their elephant owners. They use them to dig for water, salt, and roots; to take the bark off trees; as levers to move fallen trees about; for carrying logs and doing other work for their human owners if they have been tamed; for show; for marking trees; as weapons; and to protect their trunks.

Unfortunately for elephants, humans value ivory — which is what we call the material that tusks are made of — very much. Thousands of elephants have been killed each year for their tusks. So many elephants are being killed in Africa that the wild elephants there will soon be extinct if something is not done right now.

Gerald Cubitt/Bruce Coleman Ltd

◀ Poachers kill elephants for their ivory tusks. Even though it is not legal for them to do this, it is hard for African governments to control them. The best way to stop poachers from killing elephants is for people around the world to refuse to buy anything made of ivory.

survive to their children.

Elephants like to live together in groups — they are social animals. The basic group is made up of 5 to 10 animals under a female leader. When several family groups join up, they form a herd. The oldest and most experienced female is the leader.

The calves are looked after by other females in the herd, not just their mothers. Males leave the herd when they are about 13 years old. They sometimes live with other males in bachelor groups and join a group of cows (female elephants) only when one of the females is ready to mate.

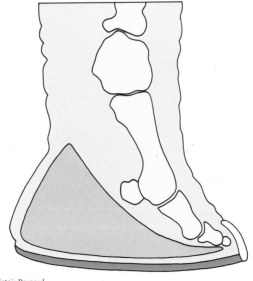

Alistair Barnard

◀ Despite their great weight, elephants walk almost on tiptoe. There is a fatty cushion behind their toes. The bottom of the foot is covered with a hoof-like skin, with only the nails visible.

# Horses and Asses

Horses and asses belong to the equid family. The Latin word for horse is "equus." The first equids lived long, long ago in North America.

## Horses

The early horses were the first hoofed animals to run on the tips of their toes across the grassy plains 20 million years ago. The first wild horses did not have such slender legs as modern-day horses. The horses alive today that look most like these early ancestors are the Przewalski's horses from Mongolia.

Horses are the largest members of the equid family, weighing 1,500 pounds (700 kg). Male horses are not much bigger than females. They do not need to be especially large because when they are fighting, they try to bite the legs of their enemies. This requires them to be quick rather than strong.

Horses can live quite well in the wild. There are wild horses on the prairies of North America, in the Camargue region of France, and in southwest Africa and Australia.

## Asses

The donkey, or burro, developed from the African wild ass. Donkeys that once carried heavy loads for gold prospectors now run wild in Death Valley, California, and the Grand Canyon, Arizona.

Not many African wild asses actually live in the wild nowadays. Those that do, live in the desert areas of Ethiopia and its neighbors. These animals are shy and hard to approach. The wild asses of Asia live in desert areas too. They look more like horses than their African relatives do. There are not many of them left in the wild either.

▶ These wild horses are galloping across grassy plains in New South Wales, Australia. They are a mixture of different breeds and came together because they strayed from home or because their owners let them go. This is why you can see horses of so many different colors, sizes, and shapes in one herd.

Jean-Paul Ferrero/Auscape International

◄ These hairy horses, with their thick legs and sturdy bodies, no longer live in the wild — only in zoos. They are Przewalski's horses and came originally from Mongolia. This species has the most in common with the ancestors of all modern horses. There is an international program for breeding them that involves the best zoos in the world.

Asses graze on what grasses they can find, the same way horses do. They also eat small amounts of leaves and twigs in times of drought. Like a female horse (mare), a mother ass carries her foal inside her body for 12 months before it is born. This means that she cannot hope to have a baby every year and still keep in step with the seasons. As a result, horses and asses do not have as many young as similar animals, such as antelopes and deer.

▼ These rare African, or Somali, asses are the ancestors of the domestic donkeys that have been tamed by humans. Asses and donkeys are better at living in dry places than horses are.

# Zebras

There are still large numbers of zebras found across Africa. The most striking feature of these mammals is their coloring — black stripes against a white, or sometimes brown, background.

Zebras weigh from 520 to 880 pounds (235 to 400 kg). They do not have as much energy as horses. The early European hunters in Africa found it easy to catch up with them on horseback. No one tried to break them in and ride them because zebras cannot go for long distances without getting tired.

## Plains zebras

Plains zebras live, as their name suggests, on grassy African plains. They form a herd with different types of antelope. A mixed group of animals like this has a better chance against the lions that try to eat them, not to mention the hyenas and wild dogs that prey on the foals. Because zebras have different eating habits than antelopes, they do not compete with them for food. The zebras can feed on the coarser parts of grass, often the seeds, which the antelopes do not want.

## Mountain zebras

Mountain zebras live in very dry areas that are almost deserts. They have rubbery hooves to help them walk over the bare rocks and dry ranges of their home.

## Grevy's zebras

A third type of zebra, called Grevy's zebra, lives in northeast Africa. Like the mountain zebra, it is found in dry, desert-like areas.

## Home sweet home

Many animals have their own areas of land, or territories, to live in. A male Grevy's zebra lives in a territory that can be as large as 4 to 6 square miles (10 to 15 square km). Within this territory, he is king. In semi-desert areas where there are only a few trees, stallions (male zebras) can see for long distances in every direction. This makes it quite easy to watch out for enemies. A stallion drops piles of its dung, or manure, to mark the boundaries of its area to make sure that other males know they are in another zebra's territory.

Most zebras live in small groups of several mares (female zebras) accompanied by a stallion. Both plains and mountain zebras live in groups like this.

▼ *These male Grevy's zebras are fighting about something serious. The stallion whose territory it is probably does not want the other one to be there. Grevy's zebras are no more closely related to other zebras than they are to horses or asses.*

K.W. Fink/Ardea London

▶ *Plains zebras are the most common kind of zebra. Also known as Burchell's zebra, they live in many areas of Africa. Can you find two zebras with identical stripe patterns? Probably not, because each zebra has its own special pattern of stripes.*

▲ This Indian rhino has a very thick skin that looks like the plates of a jointed suit of armor.

# Rhinoceroses

The rhino, as this mammal is usually known, is famous for the one or two horns it carries on its snout. From the earliest days in their history, rhinos have been large. One of their ancestors, Indricotherium, was the largest land mammal that has ever lived. Five species of rhino survive today.

## African rhinos

There are two species of African rhino, the black and the white. The way they feed is different. The white rhino grazes — it has a big head and wide lips. This makes it easy for it to crop short grasses. The black rhino browses on different types of plants. It has a hooked upper lip that is good for pulling branch tips into its mouth.

Although they are called "black" and "white," there is really not much difference between their two skin colours. Both species of rhino are basically gray. It is likely that the first white rhinos seen by explorers from Europe had been wallowing in pale soil and looked white enough to be given this name. Both white and black rhinos have two horns.

The white rhino is much bigger than the black. It is the third-largest land mammal, after the African and Asian elephants. Because it is a good-tempered beast, the white rhino was nearly wiped out after hunters developed bullets strong enough to pierce through its thick skin.

White rhinos like living in groups of 3 to 10 animals — some are young, and some are females without calves.

Females with calves move about by themselves but enjoy a friendly horn wrestle with females of another group if they meet them. Each male rhino lives by himself.

Black rhinos are less sociable. They are well known for charging at any humans who intrude onto their territory. Their puffing noises sound like a steam train. This behavior, combined with the thick bush in which the animals live, kept most hunters away until recently.

## Asian rhinos

There are three species of Asian rhinoceros. One species, the Sumatran rhinoceros, has two horns, while the Indian and the Javan rhinoceroses have only one horn.

The Sumatran rhino is a rather hairy animal and quite small for a rhinoceros. It browses in the forests of its mountain home in Sumatra and other parts of Southeast Asia.

The Indian rhino has folds on its skin that look like armor. It grazes in the swampy grasslands of India and spends

P. Jeans/Australasian Nature Transparencies

a lot of its time wallowing in ponds.

The Javan rhino browses on the leaves, twigs, and branches of its forest home. It is one of the rarest species of animal. There are only about 60 alive today, and they live in a reserve on the island of Java. Not much is known about the way they behave.

▲ The black rhinoceros has a hooked lip that is useful for pulling leaves into its mouth.

## Rhino horns for sale

Rhino horns are worth large amounts of money. Hunters cannot resist the lure of the wealth that will be theirs if they sell these horns. The horns are used as medicine in countries such as China and its neighbors. They are also used as dagger handles. Because so many rhinos are being killed for their horns, they are in danger of dying out altogether. It has been suggested that rhinos should be bred and kept in zoos, but many people concerned with conservation think that every effort should be made to keep them living in the wild.

▶ These black rhino horns were collected by African wildlife authorities. It has been suggested that in order to save the black rhinos, the governments of the countries they live in should take the horns from the

Anthony Bannister/NHPA

living animals. Then poachers would stop killing them, because rhinos are not worth much to them without horns.

# Hippopotamuses

Jane Burton/Bruce Coleman Ltd

The word "hippopotamus" comes from the ancient language of Latin and, before that, from Greek. It means "horse of the river." Hippos, as they are usually known, are closely related to pigs. They live in Africa and eat only grasses and other plants.

### Life in the water

Hippos are not designed to run fast on land. They spend most of their time in the water — this is what they are best suited for. They protect their babies from enemies, such as crocodiles, by keeping close together in a group. Hippos only come out of the water at night, when they wander about feeding on patches of short grass.

Hippos need to live in the water so that their skin does not dry out in the hot, sticky climate of their home. Such thick skin can be useful, though, and acts as armor when they need to protect themselves. Hippos use their short, sharp tusks when they are fighting.

### Pygmy hippos

The pygmy hippo does not look like other hippos. It is smaller, its legs are longer, and it does not have as much webbing between its toes. Pygmy hippos are 5½ feet (1.6 m) long and weigh 500 pounds (230 kg). Ordinary hippos are 10½ feet (3.4 m) long and weigh 5,300 pounds (2,400 kg).

Pygmy hippos live in the moist forests and swamps of West Africa. They do a lot of wallowing in water like their bigger relatives.

▲ *The pygmy hippo is about ten times lighter than the ordinary sort. While large hippos are herbivores (plant-eaters), scientists do not know much about the eating habits of the pygmy hippo.*

◄ *Open wide and say "Aah"! This hippo gives a huge yawn after a busy day wallowing among the water plants.*

Jonathan Scott/Planet Earth Pictures

◄ *These hippos are spending the day together in the water. When the sun sets at night, each hippo comes out and finds its own path to a good place to graze. Along the path are piles of its dung, or manure, left there to mark its territory. Hippos return to the water when the sun rises in the morning. These large mammals will not attack humans unless the humans try to hurt them or intrude on their marked paths.*

▲ Vicuñas live in the wild, high in the Andes Mountains of South America. They are the smallest members of the camel family. Closely related to the llama, the vicuña has a long neck, long legs, and no hump.

# Camels

The first camels lived millions of years ago in North America. At first they were quite small, but they gradually developed into huge, giraffe-like animals. They died out in North America during the Ice Ages, but the ones that had spread to South America, Europe, Asia, and North Africa managed to survive the ice.

## Bactrian camels and dromedaries

Bactrian camels have two humps. They live in central Asia. Dromedaries have one hump and are found in northern Africa, in Middle Eastern countries such as Saudi Arabia, and in the deserts of Australia.

Both the dromedary and the Bactrian

camel are about 7 feet (2 m) high at the hump. They weigh about 1,200 pounds (550 kg). Camels have a long gestation period. Their babies are large and well developed when they are born.

Wild Bactrian camels still live in the deserts of northwest China and Mongolia, and more than 25,000 dromedaries run wild in the deserts of Australia. The wild Australian ones were once tame, but their owners left them to roam free and they have been doing this ever since.

The camel family has always been important to people. Millions of camels are tamed and are used by humans for carrying heavy loads and traveling through the desert. They also provide milk to drink and wool for clothing.

## South American camels

Four species of camel live in South America: the vicuña, the guanaco, the llama, and the alpaca. They all are smaller than their relatives the Bactrian camels and the dromedaries. South American camels do not have humps.

The llama and alpaca have been tame for thousands of years. The vicuña and guanaco still live in the wild. Vicuñas used to be hunted for their beautiful golden coats, but they are now protected.

## True or false?

A camel's hump stores water for long journeys across the desert. False! A camel's hump consists of fat. Camels can draw on this extra source of energy when plants are scarce.

## Some like it hot!

The Bactrian camel and the dromedary are both famous for being able to live in very hot, dry places. They can go for long periods of time — sometimes up to 10 months — without needing water, and they feed on dry, thorny desert plants. Camels can travel long distances when they sense faraway rain and green pastures.

Lee Lyon/Bruce Coleman Ltd

◄ *Dromedaries, or camels with one hump, live in groups just like their two-humped relatives.*

57

# Large Deer

There are 39 species in the deer family. They live in many parts of the world where there are woody plants to eat. The reindeer is the only deer that doesn't need this sort of food. It lives on the flat, treeless plains (tundra) of the Arctic, where only grasses and low shrubs grow.

▼ One of the largest of the living deer, the wapiti lives in the northwestern part of North America. Its coat is darker in winter than in summer, which is unusual for an animal that lives in the snow. During the mating season, the wapiti makes a very high whistling call that sounds like a bugle.

## What are antlers anyway?

Deer are best known for their antlers, which grow and are shed each year. The biggest antlers that have ever been seen had an amazing span of 12 feet (3.5 m) and weighed just under 110 pounds (50 kg). This fine pair of antlers belonged to an Irish elk, a species that has died out.

Antlers are different from horns. Horns are made of the same substance as hair and claws and are meant to last as long as their owner does. Antlers are made of bone. They grow and then fall

David Kirshner

off each year. While the new antlers are growing, they have a covering of skin called velvet to protect them. When the antlers have finished growing, the velvet peels off, or the deer rubs it off. In most cases, the larger the deer, the larger and more complicated its antlers are.

◀ *Reindeer, or caribou, have enormous antlers with many branches, often with webs of bone between the branches. The reindeer is the only type of deer in which both males and females have antlers.*

David Kirshner

## Why are antlers so large?

It is thought that the size of a male deer's antlers has something to do with the safety of its young ones. Because deer rely on running to escape from their enemies, it is important that the young ones are as big and mature as they can possibly be when they are born. The mothers must supply them with large amounts of the richest milk so that they grow fast.

While the mother stores food and energy in her body to give to her young, the male saves a similar amount to put toward growing the biggest and best antlers he can. The female with the best milk will choose the male with the biggest antlers for mating. They will have big babies that can run fast soon after they are born and so have a better chance of surviving.

It turns out that the Irish elk — which had the biggest antlers — were also the best runners ever known among the deer. And the reindeer, with the biggest antlers of all living deer, are not only the best runners but also have the biggest babies and the richest milk.

▼ *The moose is the largest species of deer alive today. It is 5 feet 7 inches to 7 feet 8 inches (1.6 to 2.3 m) tall at its shoulder and towers above people.*

David Kirshner

# Giraffes and Okapis

There are only two species of giraffe alive today. One is the okapi, which lives in the forests of tropical Africa. It is like the giraffes that were alive millions of years ago. The other species is the huge and more familiar giraffe, which lives on the open plains of Africa.

David Kirshner

▲ *People from Europe did not know that the okapi existed until 1900. It is a very secretive animal, and we don't know much about its way of life. The pattern and color of its body give the okapi a perfect camouflage, making it almost invisible among the trees and vines of its rain forest home.*

### Giraffes

Because they feed on the green leaves of trees, giraffes have a good supply of food all through the year. They do not need to wait for a particular season when grasses grow before they can mate and have babies. They can reproduce at any time during the year.

Also because of this plentiful food supply, giraffes can grow very large. Male giraffes are about 16 feet (5 m) from their hooves to the tips of their horns. They weigh about 3,000 pounds (1,350 kg). Females are a little smaller than this. The babies are very large and mature when they are born.

Even the head of a male giraffe is big. The male uses its skull as a club for fighting, and the skin over the skull grows very thick, like armor, to protect it.

### Okapis

The okapi is much smaller than its relative the giraffe. It is about 7 feet (2 m) long, 5 feet (1.5 m) tall, and weighs 500 pounds (230 kg). It feeds on the leaves and twigs of the tropical rain forests in Africa.

Hans Reinhard/Bruce Coleman Ltd

▶ *These giraffes are running at a steady pace across the dry plains of their African home. Even though their bodies are an odd shape, they are good runners.*

# Pronghorns

$P$ronghorns are like gazelles. They chew their cuds and are often called antelopes, even though they are not really antelopes at all. These strikingly colored mammals live in groups on the plains of North America.

## Life in the fast lane

Pronghorns are very fast runners and do not get tired easily. Their bodies are suited to speed. They have a very light build without much fat, and large lungs and heart. Pronghorns can run the fastest of all the mammals in North America — about 50 mph (85 km/h) over a short distance. Even over quite long distances, they can keep up a good, fast pace.

The pronghorn young are born large.

It is most common for a female to have twins. The babies grow fast and soon become adults. Adult pronghorns are about 3 feet (87 cm) high at the shoulder and weigh 100 to 160 pounds (47 to 70 kg). Unlike giraffes, which can live for 25 years, pronghorns have a short life — about 10 years.

The branched outer covering, or sheath, of a pronghorn's horns is shed after the mating season each year and grows back the following year. The females can also grow short horns.

## Follow me

The pronghorn lives in herds on the open plains of North America. It escapes its enemies — such as coyotes — by running away as fast as it can. Each pronghorn has a white patch on its rump — the "follow me" marker. If a pronghorn scents danger, it runs, and the bobbing marker on its rump acts as a warning to the others. The last ones to run are the most likely to be caught. So it pays to run first and fast!

▶ The pronghorn lives in North America and was once hunted by Indian tribes on the Great Plains. Pronghorns are the fastest animals in North America.

David Kirshner

# Cattle and Oxen

Cattle and oxen belong to the bovid family. The word "bovid" comes from the Latin word for "ox." This family has about 107 species, including cattle, oxen, goats, sheep, gazelles, antelopes, gnus (wildebeests), hartebeests, and many others.

## Widespread mammals

All bovids graze, chew their cuds, and have horns that usually last throughout their lives. They live in all parts of the world and in many different climates, from hot deserts to snowy mountains. The only two continents that do not have native bovid species are Australia and South America. The species that live in these places were introduced from other continents.

Most species of livestock that are important to humans for food and clothing belong to the bovid family. These include cows, sheep, and goats. Their meat tastes so good because these animals eat only grasses.

▶ There's safety in numbers! Members of the bovid family use their hollow horns as weapons. This herd of wildebeests, or brindled gnus, migrates across the African plains between Kenya and South Africa once each year. Because there are so many of them traveling together, not many animals dare to attack.

Jonathan Scott/Planet Earth Pictures

▶ The musk ox is really more closely related to goats than to cattle. Its horns are used in head-butting competitions with other goats. They are also used to defend against enemies. The musk ox's dense, shaggy coat protects it from the intense cold of the Arctic tundra.

▲ This large animal trudging up a mountain is a yak. It is a kind of wild ox that lives in the highlands of Tibet. The yak, like the musk ox, has a thick, shaggy coat with the hairs matted together underneath. This protects the yak from the cold of the Himalaya Mountains. It also makes warm clothes for the people who share these mountains with yaks.

David Kirshner

◀ This gaur, or Indian bison, is a species of huge cattle that lives in the forests of India. Its coat is much smoother than the shaggy coat of the American bison.

David Kirshner

63

▲ This gerenuk munches away contentedly, apparently uninterested in the nearby bird's nest. Although other gazelles are able to stand on their hind legs, the gerenuk is the only one that can walk around like this.

# Antelopes and Gazelles

Antelopes are bovids with delicate bodies that live mainly in Africa and Asia. Gazelles are small antelopes known for their graceful movements and for their large, bright eyes.

David Kirshner

▲ ▶ *The colorful bongo (above) is a rare antelope from Africa. The Thompson's gazelle (right) is a common sight on the African plains.*

David Kirshner

David Kirshner

◀ *The Indian antelope is also called the blackbuck. This is a bit odd because it is only the most dominant males that are black. The other males and the females are brown.*

▶ *The giant sable antelope (far right) is a very rare mammal. It and the gemsbok (right) live in the wetter parts of the African plains.*

David Kirshner

David Kirshner

# Glossary

**AMPHIBIAN**: An animal that starts its life in the water and lives on land as an adult.

**ANTLER**: One of two hard horns on the head of a male deer and other animals.

**BLOWHOLE**: A nostril on top of a whale's head.

**BLUBBER**: The fat of a whale or a similar sea animal.

**CARNIVORE**: An animal that eats mainly meat.

**COLD-BLOODED**: Having a body temperature that changes as the temperature of the surrounding air or water changes.

**CRUSTACEAN**: A type of animal, such as a crab or crayfish, with a hard shell instead of a skeleton, that usually lives in water.

**CUD**: Food that cattle and some other animals return from stomach to mouth to chew a second time.

**ECOLOGIST**: A scientist who studies the relationship between living things and their environment.

**ENVIRONMENT**: The physical conditions of a place, such as weather, water, and vegetation.

**EQUATOR**: The imaginary circle around the Earth, halfway between the poles, where the climate is usually hot and wet.

**EXTINCT**: No longer existing.

**FAMILY**: A group of animals that have many things in common.

**FLUKE**: One of the triangular parts of a whale's tail.

**FOSSIL**: The remains of a plant or animal from long ago, preserved as rock.

**GENUS**: A group of animal species with many features in common, or a single distinct species.

**GESTATION PERIOD**: The time it takes for the young of placental mammals and marsupials to develop inside the mother before they are born.

**GLAND**: A part of the body that produces a substance used in another part of the body.

**GUARD HAIRS**: The coarse outer hairs that make up an animal's coat and protect the softer hairs underneath.

**HERBIVORE**: An animal that eats plants.

**HIBERNATE**: To hide away and sleep through winter.

**HORMONE**: A chemical substance made by a gland in the body that travels through the blood and affects other parts of the body.

**ICE AGE**: The time during which most of the Northern Hemisphere was covered by great sheets of ice.

**INVERTEBRATE**: An animal without a backbone.

**KRILL**: A small crustacean, like a shrimp.

**MANURE**: Animal waste.

**MARSUPIAL**: A mammal that keeps and feeds its young in a pouch.

**MATRIARCH**: The female leader of a family group.

**MIGRATE**: To change the place of living at regular times each year, as some whales do.

**MOLAR**: A tooth found at the back of the mouth suited for grinding up food.

**MOLLUSK**: An animal with a soft body, a hard shell, and no backbone, such as a snail or an octopus.

**MONOTREME**: An egg-laying mammal.

**MOLT**: To lose or throw off old fur or skin.

**NOCTURNAL**: Active by night.

**NUTRIENT**: A substance that provides the body with food and energy.

**OMNIVORE**: An animal that eats animals and plants.

**ORDER**: A group of animal families.

**PAMPAS**: A great area of grassy plains at the foot of the Andes Mountains in South America.

**PLACENTA**: The organ that gives food and oxygen to a baby in its mother's womb.

**PLANKTON**: Tiny plants and animals that float in water.

**POLLUTION**: Products that make the air, the sea, and the land dirty and unsuitable for living things to grow.

**PREDATOR**: An animal that hunts another animal as food.

**PREY**: An animal hunted for food by another.

**PRIMATE**: Any mammal of the group that includes humans, apes, and monkeys.

**PRIMITIVE**: Being the earliest in existence.

**REPTILE**: An animal that is covered in scales, breathes air through lungs, and whose body heat changes as the temperature of the surrounding air or water changes.

**SHELLFISH**: An animal that is not a fish but lives in the water and has a shell.

**SPECIES**: The basic category that scientists use to classify animals.

**TERRITORY**: Land thought of as belonging to a particular animal or group of animals.

**TUNDRA**: A treeless Arctic plain where mosses, lichens, and dwarf plants grow.

**TUSK**: The very long tooth, usually one of a pair, that certain animals such as the elephant and walrus have.

**UMBILICAL CORD**: The tube that connects an unborn baby to the lining of its mother's womb and through which food passes.

**UNDERFUR**: The soft fur that lies closest to the skin of some mammals.

**VERTEBRATE**: An animal with a backbone.

**WARM-BLOODED**: Having a body temperature that remains constant, within certain limits.

**ZOOLOGIST**: A scientist who studies animal life.

# How Scientists Group Mammals

The world has a lot more mammals than are shown in this book. Did you know there are about 4,300 kinds of mammals, both large and small?

To keep track of all these creatures, scientists have a special way of grouping them using Latin names. These different groups are called species, genus, family, order, and class. For example, the African elephant is known as the species africana, which belongs to the genus Loxodonta, which belongs to the family Elephantidae, which belongs to the order Proboscidea. This way, every single type of animal on Earth can be identified by its Latin name.

All mammals belong to the "class" called Mammalia. Below is a list of the orders in the Mammalia class. Some examples are listed for each order.

**Monotremata**
Spiny anteaters (echidnas), platypuses

**Marsupialia**
Opossums, wombats, koalas, kangaroos

**Edentata**
Anteaters, sloths, armadillos

**Insectivora**
Shrews, moles, hedgehogs

**Scandentia**
Tree shrews

**Dermoptera**
Flying lemurs

**Chiroptera**
Bats

**Primates**
Monkeys, apes, humans

**Carnivora**
Dogs, bears, cats, seals

**Cetacea**
Whales, dolphins

**Sirenia**
Dugongs, manatees

**Proboscidea**
Elephants

**Perissodactyla**
Horses, tapirs, rhinoceroses

**Hyracoidea**
Hyraxes

**Tubulidentata**
Aardvarks

**Artiodactyla**
Pigs, hippopotamuses, camels, deer, cattle

**Pholidota**
Pangolins

**Rodentia**
Beavers, squirrels, mice, rats, porcupines

**Lagomorpha**
Pikas, rabbits

**Macroscelidea**
Elephant shrews

# Index